SIMPLE MACHINES
Pulleys

by Kay Manolis

BELLWETHER MEDIA • MINNEAPOLIS, MN

Note to Librarians, Teachers, and Parents:

Blastoff! Readers are carefully developed by literacy experts and combine standards-based content with developmentally appropriate text.

Level 1 provides the most support through repetition of high-frequency words, light text, predictable sentence patterns, and strong visual support.

Level 2 offers early readers a bit more challenge through varied simple sentences, increased text load, and less repetition of high-frequency words.

Level 3 advances early-fluent readers toward fluency through increased text and concept load, less reliance on visuals, longer sentences, and more literary language.

Level 4 builds reading stamina by providing more text per page, increased use of punctuation, greater variation in sentence patterns, and increasingly challenging vocabulary.

Level 5 encourages children to move from "learning to read" to "reading to learn" by providing even more text, varied writing styles, and less familiar topics.

Whichever book is right for your reader, Blastoff! Readers are the perfect books to build confidence and encourage a love of reading that will last a lifetime!

This edition first published in 2010 by Bellwether Media, Inc.

No part of this publication may be reproduced in whole or in part without written permission of the publisher. For information regarding permission, write to Bellwether Media, Inc., Attention: Permissions Department, Post Office Box 19349, Minneapolis, MN 55419.

Library of Congress Cataloging-in-Publication Data
Manolis, Kay.
   Pulleys / by Kay Manolis.
      p. cm. — (Blastoff! readers. Simple machines)
   Includes bibliographical references and index.
   Summary: "Simple text, full color photographs, and illustrations introduce beginning readers to the basic principles of pulleys. Developed by literary experts for students in grades 2 through 5"—Provided by publisher.
   ISBN 978-1-60014-324-3 (hardcover : alk. paper)
   1. Pulleys—Juvenile literature. I. Title.

TJ1103.M35 2010
621.8—dc22   2009008270

Contents

What Is a Pulley?

Do you ever wonder how a flag gets to the top of a flagpole? Someone uses a **pulley** to raise it to the top. A pulley is a **simple machine**.

A simple machine has few or no moving parts. Pulleys move objects such as flags up, down, or sideways. These objects are called **loads**.

Moving a load from one place to another is called **work**. Work is easier with simple machines. You use **force** when you do work. Force causes things to start moving, stop moving, or change direction.

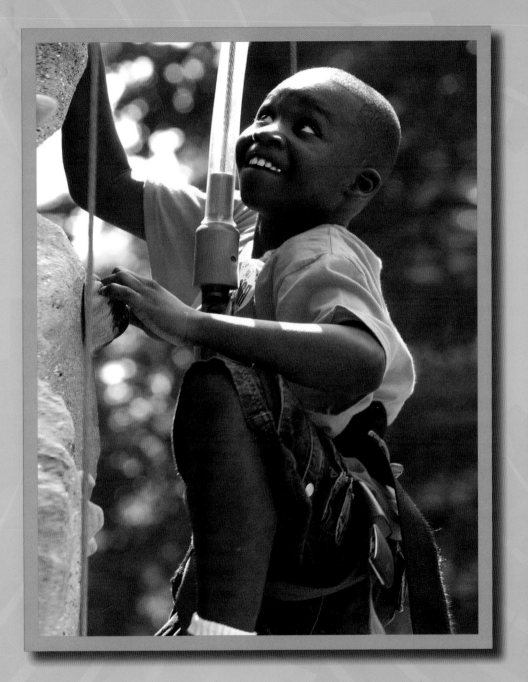

You use force when you grab rocks to climb. The amount of force you use to do a job is called **effort**.

How Pulleys Work

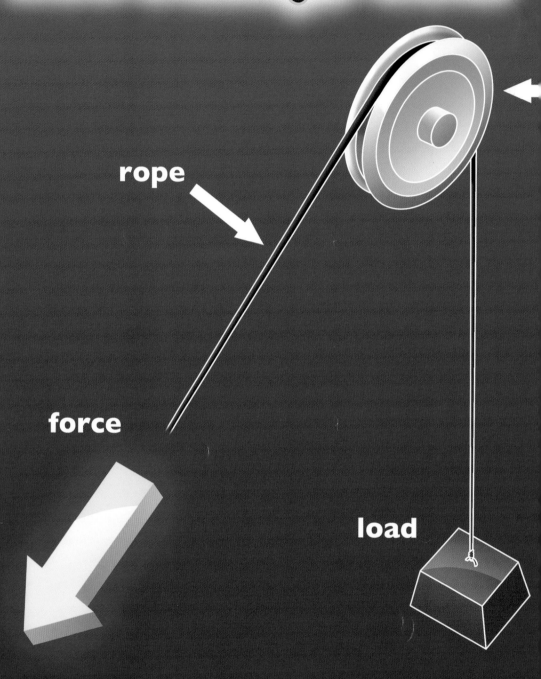

rope

force

load

wheel

A pulley uses a rope and a grooved wheel to move a load. The rope moves freely over the wheel. One end of the rope or the pulley attaches to the load. A person or machine pulls on one end of the rope. Pulleys make work easier in two ways. They either change the direction of the force or they reduce the effort needed to do a job.

fun fact

The grooved wheel in a pulley is also called a sheave.

Types of Pulleys

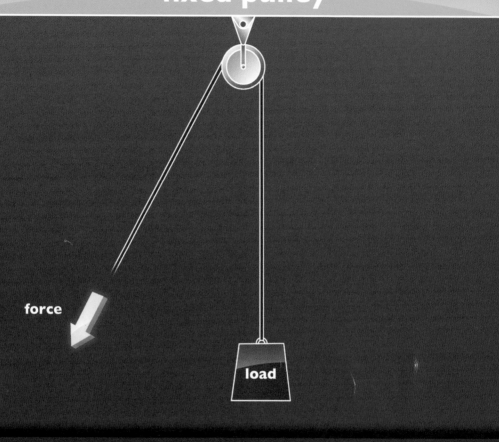

force

load

There are three kinds of pulleys. **Fixed pulleys** attach to a place above the load, such as the ceiling.

One end of the rope passes over the pulley's wheel and attaches to the load beneath it. You pull down on the other end of the rope. This turns the wheel and raises the load.

Fixed pulleys change the direction of force. You pull down on a rope to lift a load up. Pulling down is easier than pulling up because you use your body weight to help you. Fixed pulleys are used to raise and lower flags on a flagpole.

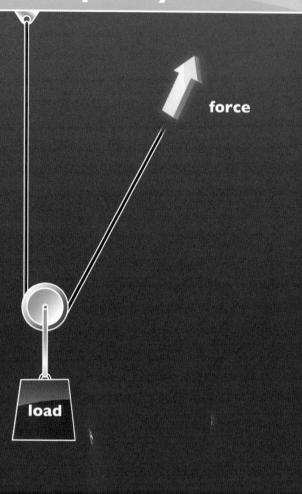

force

load

A **movable pulley** attaches to the load. When the load moves, the pulley moves with it. One end of the rope attaches to an anchored place above the pulley.

The other end of the rope passes under the wheel and back up again. You pull up on this end of the rope to raise the load.

! fun fact

The first elevator was built in France in 1743. Passengers had to tug on pulley ropes to raise and lower the elevator.

pulley

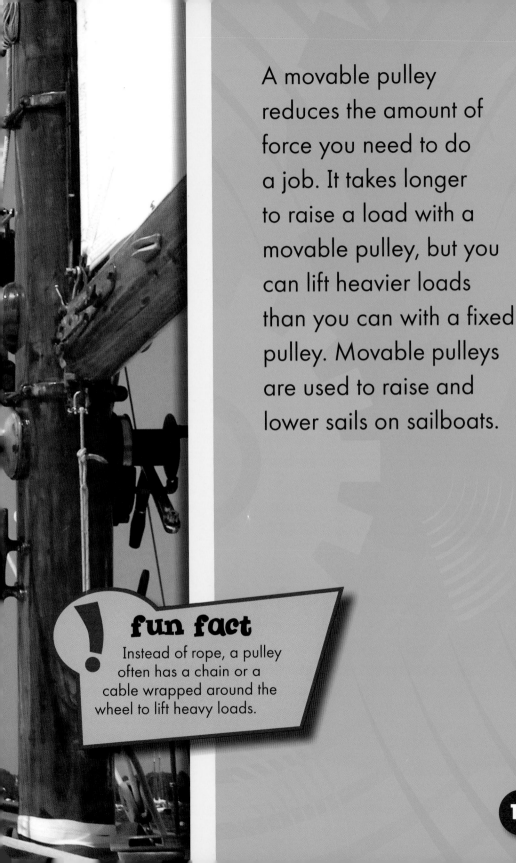

A movable pulley reduces the amount of force you need to do a job. It takes longer to raise a load with a movable pulley, but you can lift heavier loads than you can with a fixed pulley. Movable pulleys are used to raise and lower sails on sailboats.

fun fact

Instead of rope, a pulley often has a chain or a cable wrapped around the wheel to lift heavy loads.

compound pulley

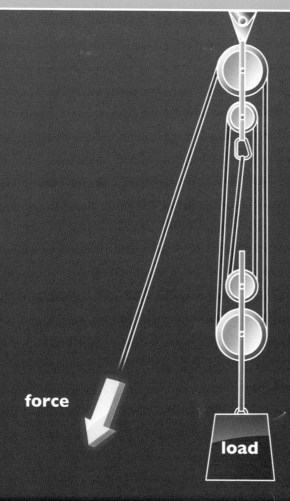

force

load

A **compound pulley** combines fixed
and movable pulleys into one pulley
system. Compound pulleys reduce the
effort needed to move a load because
the work is spread over more pulleys.

Compound pulleys lift loads that are too heavy for a single fixed pulley or movable pulley to lift. **Winches** and cranes use compound pulleys to lift heavy equipment.

Pulleys and Complex Machines

pulleys

Pulleys are often parts of **complex machines**.
A complex machine is made of two or more
simple machines that work together.

A car is a complex machine that uses pulleys. When a car's engine starts, the pulleys inside it turn at a high speed. This sends power to the wheels. The spinning wheels move the car forward!

Glossary

complex machine—a machine made of two or more simple machines that work together

compound pulley—a combination of fixed and movable pulleys that make up one pulley system

effort—the amount of force needed to move an object from one place to another

fixed pulley—a pulley that is attached to one place above a load; it changes the direction of force.

force—a push or pull that causes an object to move, change its direction, or stop moving

load—an object moved by a machine

movable pulley—a pulley that is attached to a load and moves with it

pulley—a simple machine that is made up of a rope or chain wrapped around a grooved wheel that is used to move loads up, down, or sideways

simple machine—a machine that has few or no moving parts

winch—a machine that lifts or pulls heavy objects; a winch uses a rope wrapped around a cylinder; the cylinder rotates to bring in or let out the rope.

work—to move a load from one place to another

To Learn More

AT THE LIBRARY
Gardner, Robert. *Sensational Science Projects with Simple Machines.* Berkley Heights, N.J.: Enslow, 2006.

Hewitt, Sally. *Machines We Use.* New York, N.Y.: Children's Press, 1998.

Oxlade, Chris. *Pulleys.* Chicago, Ill.: Heinemann, 2003.

ON THE WEB
Learning more about simple machines is as easy as 1, 2, 3.

1. Go to www.factsurfer.com.

2. Enter "simple machines" into the search box.

3. Click the "Surf" button and you will see a list of related Web sites.

With factsurfer.com, finding more information is just a click away.

Index

The images in this book are reproduced through the courtesy of: Lebanmax, front cover; Yui, pp. 4-5, Erik Isakson / Getty Images, p. 6; Tom Worner / Associated Press, p. 7; Jon Eppard pp. 8-9, 10, 14, 18; Peter Jones/ Alamy, p. 11; Tetra Images / Getty Images, pp. 12-13; Celia Mannings / Alamy, p. 15; Laura Stone, pp. 16-17; Alan Smillie, p. 19; Charles Turner, p. 20; Niklas Johansson, p. 21.